# Footprints of the Heart

An anthology of poetry by students
at the University of Johannesburg

First published in 2018 by Botsotso
In association with the University of Johannnesburg (UJ)

Bostotso
Box 30952
Braamfontein
2017
botsotso@artslink.co.za
www.botsotso.org.za

University of Johannesburg
31 Nind St
Doornfontein
2028
dfcarts@uj.ac.za
www.uj.ac.za/arts

ISBN: 978-1-990922-53-4

Editor: Quaz Roodt
Editorial assistance: Allan Kolski Horwitz
Layout and design: Vivienne Preston

## INTRODUCTION

Poetry is probably one of the last things that crossed Malcolm Forbes' mind when he said, 'Putting pen to paper lights more fire than matches ever will'. As the publisher of Forbes magazine, it was more likely that he was referring to the power of his magazine to influence the business world than drawing parallels with the fire ignited within us when we are given a means to give shape to a range of complex feelings, thoughts and opinions through poetry.

At the University of Johannesburg (UJ), where poetry is part of the student culture, we are indeed lighting fires with our words. In a time when tensions in the political, economic and social arenas run high, outlets such as these offer great value. Every year, hundreds of students attend the Izimbongi Poetry Festival to see the world through the eyes of the critics, visionaries, and the deep thinkers of their time. The festival is a culmination of weekly poetry workshops and monthly slams – a rigorous process – to finalize the 'best of the best' festival line-up and so meet the standard of the professional spoken word artists who are also featured on the programme.

UJ Arts & Culture is tremendously proud to publish this collection of poetry written and performed by students at the Izimbongi Poetry Festival over the past five years. The collection beautifully brings together an array of pieces dealing with a wide range of themes including loss – lamenting a relationship that ended, an absent parent or the void left by death. I commend the student-contributors, the UJ Arts & Culture champion of this project – Mzwandile Maphumulo – and Quaz Roodt, who expertly coached the students and curated the anthology.

*Pieter Jacobs*
*HEAD: ARTS & CULTURE*
*UNIVERSITY OF JOHANNESBURG*

# CONTENTS

## Refiloe Khumalo
Poet, actress, student.

## Jazz Man

My backbone is a funeral song/
a collection of Cathedral type requiems.
Trees slide under the music/through the breeze/between turgid
mountains
and heavy hopes of laboured incantation/till Jazz man appears!

With two strong ears/he hears the moan of ancient sunsets
tune the raw sounds of love making in between saffron sheets
on poisonous nights/ lonely with alcohol.

Jazz men aren't really all that jazz/just extra
extra spice on your plate in case you thought stomaching a masala
stew wouldn't burn
your blood cold/rapturous evening firework display
ballerinas toe-to-toe/grunting their teeth at their slice of the
fire/
ready to become dragons.

Jazz men aren't all that jazz/ just more.

More turmeric in the scales/
more cinnamon in the brass/
less lemon zest in the strings/
more butterflies in the soup/
more colours procreating/
more blue/ that vast sky of the Karoo/
melting blackdrop/ starry fingers.

Galaxy Tupperware (better not give that shit away)
it cost too much to hold oceans and trombones all at a blow.
Give them one note/stave seamed/orchestrated tapestry.
Jazz man will show you/ how to do this/ he does & will do.

Jazz men/sinking maelstroms/
water drinks itself thirsty/
you should be a moment of dark desert/
haste love/ trickling sigh of relief.


Jazz men are:
Trembling wings/coward enough to fly.
Fermenting dust/drizzling soft stones on dry mountains.
When I hear your breathing/unmothered rhythms roam wild
amongst the aching thunders trying to find a bruised music/
I will be a dam for you/ open the earth up
ease me into your sorrows/ until I'm pressed tight into your blood.


Until then, the stare of a naked song will sculpture your shadow for
me:
shades of purple on amethyst/ massage the memory of atasi
flowers/
royal smell of Krishna/you, forbidden ketaki
look like pãtal/ petals from nature's hair.


Jazz men/I have carved for us a sarcophagus.
We will fall in love again/ in the afterlife.
Coffin texts with poems/ our flesh will be eaten by words/
a death I am ready to drench my lungs in/ for now, I will write
letters to you/ on papyrus/
give them to Vishnu & Lakshmi/
they will know how to open a galaxy.


Read the letter.
It will teach you how to hold a lotus;
three halves of a jazz song.

## Cosmic Entrances

Hello comes
too soon sometimes
like 1652 handshakes
when you haven't brushed your ego out

eye bags carry whole red giants in their stellar exit
face, with patches of nebula
still, I am Orion Nebula
Queen of all nebulae
I am two light years away from your deadly hello!

## Celestial Assignment

Sun is out.
Toes are dangling.
Double bass is giving birth.
It's a boy!
Sax needs some love.
Old songs!

The balcony is a size too small to fit our adventures.
He curls his beard into a secret.
We sit, wonder if the other will ask about the sound around his bed.

Why are there no curtains?
Why won't you hide the universe?
He pulls another breath and says he's not alone.

## Asylum Seeking Skin

When your skin feels heavy
peel it off
steep it in hot water, parboil until perfectly cooked
hang it over white picket fences
on a hot day roast it, maybe host a braai

When your skin feels heavy
remember that sunlight goes there to die
her cremated lovers smothered over your body
her remains remind you that you are a living graveyard
hollow fantasy

They will stuff you into coffins
push you whole into a colony of death
when you cry, they will beat you
until your yoke is three times the weight of your tears

Then dip you in powdered white noise
pan-fry you in Joburg city grime
garnish the wounds with fancy bandages
pungent Himalayan scents
used to wipe the smell of anxiety on Jesus' feet
wrap you up in old satin nightgowns the Mrs gave to the less
fortunate

When your skin feels heavy
add a pinch of salt
trace the lines on your palms to your ancestors
tell them your skin did not get the memo

When your skin feels heavy
the white lady, caressing your right shoulder, tells you nothing is for free
ask her:  "How much did you pay for your skin"?

## Hold Your Sunrise

Does he not know that I am stark moonless next to him?
Rags, from sunlight's ashes brewing in fire.
Twilight's poem on the bottom of my shoe.
Tapping.
Clicking.
Thrusting.
This is how shreds of fire walk on the pavement.

Does he not know I have bite size volcanoes, he can baptize
his teeth into every time he thinks he's just too cool?
This boy!
He doesn't know I shed blood with Jezebel.
Danced to jazz music on 12th fuck your bullshit Avenue after, corner
& curve your ass back to where you belong.

Someone should tell him not to come too close to the glory of God.
Not to enter the holy of holies unsanctioned.
I'm sunshine dipped in hell too hot for you.

Hold your sunrise.
You're not ready for this.

## Phumelelokuhle Ngidi
Poet, film maker.

## An Excursion with Melancholia

Don't come look for me.
I'll be gone,
Leaving a hollow house
With shredded papers of unfinished poems.

Don't come look for me.
I'm torn
Between churches and liquor stores
Whirling through songs of broken men and vagabonds.

Don't come look for me.
I'll be gone
To distant gardens where trees
Speak to each other in clicks,
Where silence affords me to think
About nothing.

Don't come look for me.
I am torn
Between the stars and the earth,
Searching
Between what is right and wrong.

Don't come look for me.
I'll be gone,
Leaving you with your trolls and goblins.
And this time I won't be there when you're falling
Into your melancholic dungeon.

Don't come look for me.
I'm torn
Between my mind and my heart.
I don't know which to listen,
I can't sleep at night.

Don't come look for me.
I'm torn.
Don't come look for me.
I'm gone.

Don't come look for me.
I'm torn
Between my mind and my heart.
I don't know which to listen,
I can't sleep at night.

Don't come look for me.
I'm torn.
Don't come look for me.
I'm gone.

## Omnipotence of Self

I have been here before
As a barrel of simmering thoughts
As tall men and women fell from grace down to earth like flickering
lightning bolts
As a woman who told her people to kill their cattle and burn all
crops
As a loincloth that covered a newborn's beginnings

I have been here before
As the sparkling eye of the mother of seven winds
As pollen dust that oozes out of the tapestry of spring
As a little boy who travelled the world and then spoke of fools for
kings
Of false prophets and their persistent dreams

I have been here before
As a black author who writes what he likes
A clasp between silhouettes and twilights
As a cosmic mermaid with fishscale-like feathers
For centuries mistaken for a shooting star, for the god-speed they
couldn't fathom
It was I who taught the rays of the sky to fondle with sky
Remnants of song that feed on memory to thrive

I have been here before
As Ukhamba – that tasted the froth of roasted corn beer
As Inkanyamba – the giant snake who scraped the skies and left all
withered
As Indaba – that carried customs like strong ancient pillars
As Inyanga – that gurgled shadows of night to help children cross
the river
As Ilanga – that kept the days bright even during the zenith of winter

I have been here before
As soil that was fertile but is now barren
As the hands of a man who woke Lazarus from the dead
As a raging phoenix through the ashes I returned

I am here now
Light encased in flesh
I never said I was poet
It just came to me
Twirling
Reminding me that I am a piece
Of that which weaved everything into being

## My Long Lost Broken Father

Father, where are you?
I've searched for you
In hovering scent of uneven jazz and grotesque blues
Plunged into mother's purple heart
Found scotching gobs, horrid and oblique puddles reflecting
You following a head of headless men into the hollow earth
Shambling
Ankles tied with flaming girth
Advancing like a chain of ants.

Father, where are you heading?
Leaving mother with towering burdens
But mother is strong; you should see her when she sings her
enchanting songs
Throngs of thistles gather round her to bond
A woman made of golden dust
One exalted by the waters and stretched skin of drums
One who breathes dance into the winds, a glory unsung.

Daytime, she clutches on burning incense
To swallow the vapour with her lungs
Eyes closed, her neck ascends to the cosmos
Hands flimsy as smoke, exuding waves
Shuddering pine cones
Where children play
Night, in her dreams she bends your pathways and embroiders
them kisses
For you to return home.

Kodwa wena baba
Uyinja, edla ezinyaweni zomlungu
Ekuseni masivuswa yinkukhu,
Usishiya nezinhliziyo ezibhodla ubuhlungu
Ugcwal'ilokishi, usaphazek'okwemvuthu
How far have you stretched yourself away from yourself?
Whose footsteps am I to follow when yours stray me away from self?

Your charred six-legged demons visit me
Making me sing songs that curl my tongue down my throat.

At night, I choke
During the day, I choke
In fright, I choke
Where angels lay, I choke.

Father, I need you
Take my hand; tell me my palms complement the grains of sand
Bluets and lilies, cotton of snow, coiling vines, and the Pleiades
My son, I'm a broken man
All life has seeped through these cracks caused by pale men
From a frozen land.

Bury the memory of me next to weeping willow trees
And write beautiful poetry of how your mother raised a king.

## Dear Woman

Death is playing hopscotch on your scars until they bleed
Creating hollow caves that go skin deep
Tying knots that will split your neck and put you to eternal sleep
Death is ignoring your heart volunteering to speak
It leaps because it's almost time to sleep
As you slip and skip one too many beats

Death is the heat oozing from your skin
As another woman's son beats you hard revealing what's within
Each fist resembling the echo of a drum as your heart beat stops like
it never had to begin
Thinking it's worth it because your life is a concoction of his rib and
God's breath
Your flesh almost tasting death
Your feet pleading with burning concrete to keep your dirty secret
When will you say enough?
When will you get mad enough?
Overwhelmed with rage enough to tell him you've had enough?
When?

You came to the party guns blazing
Your head flickering above the 9th cloud, you been blazing
But see the marriage of gravity and his strength will make sure you
come back down hard
Ain't no escaping
Just as the earth keeps rotating
Your head keeps spinning and you're losing direction
Because your mouth has muted the inner man speaking

Woman, it's time to wet that clay
Get on the moulding tray and start fixing
No more crying, start talking

The bones were dried up without breath until Ezekiel learnt the fine art of speaking
Sorry to burst your bubble but #MenAreTrash will not send vibrations
Into your lifeless bones so as to revive you

Fight back while the soil is still beside you
You've got to trust you
You are a brown buttered force
And your tongue is a burning blade
Wonderfully and fearfully made
Pure enough to evoke life
While carrying the world on your back
You are strong
You are bold
You are . . . WOMAN

## Sithembiso Mokuwa
Poet – winner of the 2017 UJ Can You Slam.

## Maboneng

Jozi, Maboneng, Jhoni
The private hospital where dreams are born
And the backroom clinic where reality aborts them
So lucid are these illusions advertised, it's a breeze for vendors to extort them
They sold us dreams and we bought them
First the architects created their own stars with lights and in the night time she came alive
With vigor, vehemence, vivacity and vibe
I saw the sights of Jozi
Shebeen queens in their liquid castles serving blacks Black Label

Now it's common for blacks to be labeled, "alcoholics"
But my ignorance saw adventures on their tables –
Knights with Strongbows were hunters of Russian bears
Or those who lacked a care
Mainly staying on long islands looking up at the sky
But alcohol really Daniels mean jack

When some of the drunkards were miners whose concerns were rendered minor
The intention was possessive not progressive
Mari kana – how did we think they'd share the gold if they called it a mine?
I guess rands and cents are points in the game
So the rich hope it stays the same while the poor beg for change
But ubaba Mbuli gave me hope

He said, "Gagashi, kwasukasukela once upon a time
There were people like Phiri, Rathebe and Masekela
Who sang songs of pain and passion like Stimela.
And there were also blacks like the Black Jacks
Who told blacks they weren't jack while jacking from blacks"

City of gold, you can't gold dig us because the gold is not under us

It's within us.

# Tshiamo 'Sir Dice' Modise

Born in Johannesburg, grew up in the remote village of Mabaalstad. A BTech Chemical Engineering Graduate, writer and lover of all art forms, he has, since 2006, been writing as a form of self-healing or what he refers to as the "art of dissolving problems in ink and leaving the solution on paper."

## Reproduction: Behind the Sins

As we wash our dirty minds
In the crazy storms of coitus
Undressing you and me to call us out
Forming unity that bares our kind

Whenever the tide of life brings unrest
Kids are the anchor to keep us at rest
In the event where the bond should fail
We'll have sinking communities to sail

And so, though it brings pleasure, like other things
Reproduction is sacred behind its sins
Through the crevices of a broken heart,
Love spies on other disasters that are just as smart

## Broken Star

You broke me into pieces of asteroids
I now float in the space you once filled
Destroying other planets that I hit on

## Off Peaknic

Hanging out online
Biting on data bundles
Flirting with the airtime
Hoping for free minutes

Emptying all my accounts
Buying bulk for discounts Thama Khomunala

## Big Boned

I am not fat, I'm big boned
yes, I like my number 23
with extra cheese and good God please don't hold back the secret recipe
I'm salivating as my blood pressures's elevating
for a delectably delicious lip-smacking treat
something face-stuffing or sweet
to be snacked after the savoury I scoff down the street
yo, deep fried fries I can choke down on the beat
but before I do, hey, I haven't upsized
upsize! upsize!
but make it a diet coke
coz I'm not fat, I'm big boned.

It's no surprise my waistline is like a bassline to some dubstep
it never really comes to end
and it's so hard to find jeans I can actually bend-in
so anything skinny is really out of the question
and let's not mention anything else I can hardly fit my ass in
like society or the cool kids at school
shirtless at the public swimming pool
a positive stigma attached to cleanliness and great hygiene
park swings, wedding rings, all for self-esteem
the first pick to the first team
my crush and their wet dreams
coz I'm not fat, I'm big boned with the means.

But for now I'll take the tracksuit pants, sir – no, the ones with the elastic
one size fits all? ridiculous! I must be one size too tall
the truth is, if my plus size were any more plus size
it would have been a multiply in your eyes

and where you see disease like obesity and gout
I doubt you've realized that as much as one learns to love oneself
others are taught to hate.

And sure it transpires into something utterly under your own
self-control
coz my mom could not wait to tell me how useless I was
my dad could not wait to get home to beat me
my uncle could not wait to touch me where he wanted
my class mates could not wait to direct their next joke
my teachers could not wait to laugh along
my community could not wait to stare and comment
media can't wait to tell me how I should look this summer
my friend cannot wait to tell me that it's not the jeans
And so . . . I run, I run.

I run from depression and suicide
I run so you cannot tell apart my tears from the sweat in my eyes
I run from diabetes in my early thirties
I run for my children whom I will not be able to pick up without
breathing heavily
I run until the salt on my wounds is the salt on my face
and while I run I feel prying eyes
remind me this is not who I am inside
and so I run to stay alive.

Yes, I run, I run for my life
I run, and this journey is long
and when it gets cold I run alone . . .
Because as I have said,
I'm not fat – I'm big boned.

## Hip Hop: The Genesis

This! this is hip hop, the Genesis:

As the nation was formed, originated by
wordsmiths, lyricists, beat makers and beat boxers
boxed beats on tape records
bound together with a bad stapler
so its paper staple, paper paper sss-staple staple
all for the sake of a lyrical art form
yet the disciples of this nation couldn't keep it together
so our generation is a regeneration of degenerating heads
but who am I as a fruit from this tree to be pointing out our own
mediocrity?
this peace-making movement through music, oh my God the
audacity
coz i too am a product of amampantsula patrons
i too bop head to motswako revelation
i too turn up despite the state of our nation
so how then amongst all the bliss
do we find the nerve to plug in politics
talk about poverty and the shortfalls of economy
corrupt government and national party
when honestly all we ever wanted to do is party!
but how could we?!
celebrate when that young celibate sister has just been raped
or someone's mom just been abused like hip hop music? get it?
i murdered it . . . I killed it, you should have seen me dawg
a sick flow kinda like all her blood on the wall
so peacemaker, peacemaker, what then inspires you?
the un-fabulous lifestyles of the un-fabulous that no one fantasizes
about?

My story.

## Judah Sipho Mhlaba

Has a National Diploma in Town and Regional Planning (UJ); was born in Limpopo, grew up in Mpumalanga and now resides in Nelspruit. Judah has always had a keen interest in the creative arts and has been writing since 1999.

## You Were There

I attended a funeral today – you were there.
People cried, halls were filled.
I still don't understand why you were there.

Preachers preached, friends *speeched*,
relatives of the deceased . . . and you were there.
Flowers towered then you collapsed as the box was lowered.

I attended a funeral today.
You were there when I died –
when I crossed through to the other side.


## Who Am I

My attempts to save myself from this world have been futile;
ideas from a great-minded body and spirit, infertile.
From idealists, ideal approaches, one idea to another –
all seem to fail or not perform according to perfectionist procedures.
Ideas grown in the mush of my brain
somewhere amongst the evil the world has dumped.
Rows and rows, scattered,
contaminated and dislodged from common sense.
How wicked will the fruit of these ideas be?
As sweet as revenge?
Have I not become the product of society dislodged from reality –
Or is reality an illusion society has perfected?

## Terrence Valashiya
Poet, writer, performer.

## Optimistic

I'm sorry
But I despise going to school on a Monday morning
I'll wake up at first light to rush to church on Sunday
Fully aware of each action as I go through the day
And unlike the blue Mondays that start the lengthy weeks
This day is sure to be spent in joy and acceptance

And then sometimes I like to stroll in the moonlight
At one with the creation, the displayed vista
Singing a symphony that rests my soul
Not forgetting to pour out my feelings on paper
Creating rhythm with my hands as I match my heartbeat
Spilling all that is felt within the heart but never uttered

And through the carnival door I observe
Oblivious to the events on show
The clouded-sunny sky as it dares me to take a challenge:
Will I fail the test of patience under its gaze
Though intensely persistent in witnessing my failure
Delayed, as I am, by a flowing river of dark, lucid water.

# Freedom?

Broken nations mother orphans:
Demented delegates, heirs to destruction
Haunted, armoured ten-year olds
Anguished minds of their bleeding mothers
Daunting the spirits of foreboding fathers

Barrels raised high
Ammunition belts on stiff shoulders
Drying blood on deafened ears
Forever hearing endless cries
Of guns and bullets

Overzealous
Defending the honour of pseudo-men
Pseudo-smiles
Ransacking families
Waging war on weaker nations

Greed seeks destruction
Of potential threats
Risks brave men
To protect reputation
For cowards in hiding
Sends soldiers to battlegrounds

And so they ravage homes of families
Force children to stand with arms
And protect a country
That will forever ransom their freedom

And then these men stand up tall
From utter pure 'nothings' to citizens
Who destroy in the name of freedom

Foreseeing threats
They desecrate homes
Make empty promises
Sacrifice lives
For a country
That will never love them.

# Welcome

Come over to the dark side . . .

The voices call with intriguing calamity
Draw you close
Heir to hell's ecstasy
Welcome to a land of no return

Then they grope with dreary hands
Whispers in the darkness
Seeping slowly into your spirit
Calling you to the shadows

And you hear the groans of tormented souls
They call you, again and again, how they call!
Something urges you on
You take a step forward then another

And this time you hear them clearly
The chant your name and nothing else


Feel at home with your dark side.

## Karabo Mogodi

Poet, student.

## Careless Dance

We lay happy on concrete melodies
waiting for the world to open doors for us

Riding high on society
chauffeured into our comfortable thoughts by their disapproval
my veins sing birth
pouring cries of growth to build a monument

I dance to these hard walls that govern brains
sing softly to the graves that comfort us
Success, Freedom and Life share blankets with humour
while I compose songs filled with broken string, wrong chords

Then I dance carelessly to the wrong side of these concrete melodies
pen mating with paper
Impregnated with the ugly truths of rhythm

Come, dance with me
I'm just
Painting freedom in life

# Where I'm From

We hallucinate
About love, laughter, peace and happiness

Where I'm from
Eruptions of pain symbolize love
Illness defines my brothers and sisters
We abduct our sibling to picnics where bullets are breast- fed
We ensure marriage is archived when they hallucinate prayers
cocooned in pain
and say, 'Until death do us part'

After metamorphosis they rupture into butterflies that feed off
sentences
like

'Do it'
'I hate you'
'You are useless'

These are:
Lullabies they sing to their genotypes
Bullets and gun shots turned into soulful jazz music

Where I'm from

The love is different
Knives are pens that turn our bodies into paper so love letters
can be written on us

Where I'm from

Scars are lessons to woman that don't allow defeat
Death is the best bedtime story for the young

Where I'm from

Females are forcefully fed off their precious areas

The river of pain shall always symbolize love
They smile and laugh
About how graceful females look when they impersonate mummies
with bandages round their faces

Where I'm from

The love is different
Our runways are decorated with black and fashionable caskets
We accessorize with unhappiness

Where I'm from

Hate is love and love is taboo
Beauty has turned into a curse
Degrees in greed are obtained more than ubuntu

Where I'm from

When the morphological structure cannot endure
We lay the soul to rest
Play its most hated songs
Serve horrible dishes

As you can see
Where I come from

The love is different.

## The Golden Girl

When I heard of her I wanted to meet her

She was the golden girl
I was the kasi boy

She was complicated
She taught me to drink
She was always awake
Man, she slept less and talked about natural selection
Abiding by principles will make you survive

So I spoiled her
She introduced me to leaves that give you that nostalgic feeling after
inhaling
She knew every trick

Her friends worshipped money
They sold their bodies
It was normal
She was always free
But to be with her I had to bypass my education

Hey wena
You will try to kiss the whole world
And not everyone has fresh breath
Sharing is caring
Where on earth do you eat a banana without pealing it off?

Sharing is caring
She stopped caring but then she shared with me
And by the way
I boxed our memories

I still miss you
There's a kid like me falling for you
You'll embrace him

She was Johannesburg
And I was a naughty kasi boy from Polokwane

## Keitumetse 'Ali' Tlhako

Born and bred in Rustenburg, raised in a huge family, Keitumetse has been writing since she was 7. It started off as small notes when she couldn't say something out loud, especially when things got emotional. Loves reading, sports, music and movies. Believes in dreaming within realistic boundaries.

## Songs About You

Songs about you usually sound

like the deep sigh of the ocean after 15:30pm
like escaping dead bodies
like crippled trees and cold coffee
the end of church hymns
the back of long queues.
Not this time though.

Not when you sing them yourself.

Not when you compose them yourself.

Not when you've realized you matter.

## Untitled 3

Success hangs on your shoulders
like anxious stars waiting for nightfall.
The skyline of the city carries the promise
that even the shadiest of days have light at the end.
And though we run like the wind, through and for it,
the city never stops coming for us:
arriving home with only your keys, or less,
lurking on the stranger's face nearby.
Nothing but our breath belongs to us.
And even that can be stolen.

## Upon Leaving

When the war comes

You will first smell the heat in your skin.
You will taste the blood in your mouth.
You will hear the door creak open.
You will feel the ending when he says he's leaving.
Then you will have peace.

But you are all the pieces you need
to rebuild yourself.

## Mondays on the Boulevard

I can describe to you what pain feels like before it hits the ground.
It is the crunch of leaves in autumn.

And though I can't mend a broken heart,
I know how to cradle you tight enough to make the pieces cling
together.
I guess that's why you only love me when I'm there,
And love me less when I am gone.

The sun sets in my eyes and every evening takes away the day.
In my solitude I drown memories of you in wine and tears.

## Sibusiso Dladla
Poet, student (Soweto Campus)

## Night

Shines in wintery hearts
Pale as autumn's thirst
We pillow-talked the willows
Velveted in blankets
Caressing woodblocks accompanying them
Into the deadliness

Outstretched in the airy man's existence
Hailing warmth
We welcomed these fellows
Our minds as shallow as our self esteem

We are not that yellow
As the eyes of the mellow-deeds
Sung by their guitars with broken strings
To tie our hopes and dreams
To their dangling foreskins

## Speak Silence

In the pit of empty stomachs celebrating freedom
As fists plummet in faith without wisdom
My heart pouts in the ring of bitter silenced ears
And while steel shivers with smooth breezes
I still bleed
For pain and anger disprove my being

Is being black the richest sin in the book of deceit?
Dry for love at the dawn of lust
Ignorance failures my heartbeat
While my heart twangs in pondering the lies of an off tune drum

Africa descend from dust that fell upon testaments and testaments
to come
Fear not metaFives in your feint margin mind
Punchlines to illiterate druggies and alcoholics in search of a fruitful
life
To paralyze verbs and slaughter your nouns

# Daniel Mahaba

Born 1st of January 1991 at Sebokeng hospital; grew up in Vaal where he attended three primary schools; namely, Atlehang in Zone 7 (1997-98), Bula Tsela in Zone 3 (1999-2001) and Modula Qhowa in Zone 11 (2002-2004). Daniel then went to Esokwazi Secondary School where he started writing kwaito in 2005. Met majita who were into hip hop the following year, began following cyphers and participating in them. When he got to Joburg, he met other guys who introduced him to poetry and to be honest he loves poetry more.

## Dissembling Care

Under the custody of your shadow she felt safe
She opened herself to you
Disclosed her breaking points
For you came across as the different one
And she hated being a day apart
Though you veiled your motives
Availed her schoolgirl fantasies
Displayed to her glaring eyes what they sought

Yes, your timely words robbed her of her logic
She bought the lies that you sold at reasonable emotional damage
With your arms coiled around her figure
Figuring an angle to enter her
She thought you two were sailing to vacant shores of forever
Given the dissembling care you assembled
She broke her promise to herself
Broke her chastity
Unaware that you were racing for street applause and player ranks

Now she rues that night and the seed that escaped a burst condom

And he?

He stalks a new victim.

## Our Obituary

Retrieve the past
Look carefully into every second
Visit the cemetery of our decease
Erect tombstones, inscribe on them 'best times'
Mummify those orgasmic moments
Then let your loneliness
Employ your mind museum
And exhibit your dull present

Indeed, commemorate conversations that depicted us as soul mates
Clone those intimate exchanges
Paste glossy posters on your bedroom walls
Protest the death of love with placards denouncing our policy of
1st Corinthians 13
So the womb of your memory may deliver happiness

Revisit March 2006
Loiter in the lane that led us to today
Remember how the rain held us hostage under your colorful
umbrella
I talked, you listened, I asked, you replied, we agreed on nothing
Therefore us depends on the end of YOU & I

Wait!
There was never us – this poem is a lie.

## Tshifhiwa Thovhakale
Poet, writer.

## Blood Soil
Revolution soil
The struggle harvest tombstone
Songs of judgement
We feed from the freedom charter
Particulars of familiar dead miners

## Our Ancestors
Our ancestors which art most feared, hallowed be thy name
Thy king has come
Thy will be done in motion as it is produced in rhythm
Give us our land, our daily bread
And forgive us negotiations, as we forgive our enslavers
And lead us not into temptation but deliver us from evil;
For thine is Azania
And Black Power
And African knowledge
Forever and ever
Amen

## Sisters
A prostituted law
The influence of demand
A broken homeland

# Mpoba Knowledge Monyeke

Or Knowledge as he is affectionately known, is a poet from Maseru, Lesotho and a UJ Alumni. He has taken part in numerous performances in and around Jozi and Maseru and is known for his deep articulate voice and love for poetry.

## Confused Minds of African Black Seeds

Black man, where is your black horizon?
Black man, where has your black pride gone?
Africans, are we still fighting for revolution?
We are confused like a teenage girl
Writing out New Year resolutions
But never living up to any of them!

Stuck between two powerful walls –
Xenophobic attacks and civil wars –
Black man, where is your black consciousness?
Our atmosphere stinks of storms of violence
Yet we sit in silence, painting rainbows
With our very own sisters' and brothers' blood.
Truly, we need our forefathers' guidance!

We embrace war like the pain
Of slave-trade, yet we still claim to be free!
Black man is brainwashed, his mind fed
With western lifestyle ideology,
Neglecting his own black thoughts
And African living methodology,
Subsequently losing his roots completely!
Insulting his black intelligence,
Spitting on his own black inheritance –
Why do we have to live in chains of violence?

Think of Steve Biko, Oliver Tambo and other African heroes!
Think of our forefathers who died resisting!
Black man, can't you see this western ideology

Only reflects 'pop-psychology'?
If we are truly free why do we have to flock at police stations?
Why do we have rape as the main talking point
On our broadcasting networks, our radio stations?
Yes, we are civilized – ugly nations without love,
Keeping GOD out of the picture, peace and harmony
Sunk into oblivion, obscured by hatred.

We are just oppressed and colonized African citizens
Segregated by borders, political parties, national flag colours
But most sadly by our own skin colour.

Let them restructure your twisted present
To offer you a fruitful future!

## Manuscripts of Knowledge

Take me on a journey through a telescopic view of history
Siyavuma makhosi sa mochonoko a binela hlophe
Le 'na nkenye lenakeng la motheo
Tebisa kepi Sesothong, fepa kelello eaka ka lioelioetla
Tsa nalane hotsoa sesiung sa tsebo e manoni

Nthute sehaeso se monate ntho ena ke
Makhea monate oa eona o kena pelong
E re le 'na ke kene khabong ho ea linakeling
Ke tle jare ak'a masasa ke lebe mangaung,
Ka bosiu ba lelingoana o mphe mekhabo-puo
Ke tle ke khabe ha boesa ke ithoka

Mpinele maele, tsebo e oele tsebeng tsaka
Sa marotholi a liphara a pula tsa molubela
Ha li ngobetsa the dry of soil of my land.
Ke anye e letsoele le mohasula
Ke imone monoana ka sokotso le mafura
La khomo ea lebese 'malihlofa
Khomo e sisang bese la mofuta tlhalefo

Nthute sehaeso se seke sa timela ke shebile
Like a receptive child sitting at ifo attentively
Listening to nkhono narrating historic stories of
Ancient Basotho nation walking through the passage of
Ntsoana-tsatsi

Embarking on a journey all the way to the mountain kingdom
The kingdom in the sky, Boroa ba Afrika
Teach me Basotho Ethics, I'm listening to you
Nthute hore; motho ke motho ka batho ba bang
Matsoho a hlatsoana, tso'ele le beta poho
Etsoe letsema ke matla,
O ka nketsang ha e hae motse
Motse ho ahoa oa morapeli – motlola thapelo!
Nthute mekhoa le maele a baholo-holo baka

Nthute sehaeso ke itsebe
Engineer words, i will write syllables
In my praise poetry and let it be carried by the wailing
Wind to recite a eulogy on top of Thaba-Bosiu
To pay homage to my forefathers
My trend-setters and my road pavers

Nthute le 'na ke tle ke tsebe ho ea
Molutsoaneng ke ilo bua le Rare
Molimo o moholo Jere, Tlhatlha-macholo
A re kolobesta ka keleli tsa mariha le hlabula
Lesotho le apereloe ke nala
Thena khoroa li ehlabe ka sefea-maeba
Khobe re hlabe ka lemao, re jele poqo ka hlanaka
Unleash the proverbial manuscripts and let me learn from you
I'm a child constantly yearning for indigenous ancient knowledge

## Footprints of the Heart

The voice of this lyricist speaks vibrantly
Through the flexible and fluent tongue of a pen,
With metaphors and similes connecting,
Intertwining and articulately portraying
Footprints of the heart.

Words pour out of the pores of my porous soul,
Painting my poems with radiant colors:
Of truth I speak to you
With the voice that shakes the lungs
In my chest, vibrates in the membranes
At the backs of our brains.

With the sand of these shores,
I weave the strings that will link your dreams.
Forget your flaws; bury the story of your sad past
But shape the land-paths that will give you glory.
Let your dreams be the footprints of your heart!

Let them nurture you.
Let them groom you.
Let them mould you.
Let them inspire you.
Let them nourish your character's finest texture.

# Ratsoana Ratsoana

Born on 3rd July 1988, a natural speaker, he participated in debate during his high school years and through hard work competed on a national level. He has grown incredibly over the years through this facility with words. Some of his achievements include being a Peer Mentor, most disciplined poet in 2009 (UJ AFRO ALPHaBETS,) Peer Buddy for UJ (2009-2010), Best Speaker of the word-athon (Vosloorus) in both 2009 and 2010.

## Let Me Show You My Dreams

Where time would stand still,
And mothers of this earth wouldn't be ill . . .

Let me show you a dream.
Where our footprints would walk side by side,
Our hands intertwined and our hearts beat as one.

Let me show you my dreams.
Where we would wonder at love,
Describe its beauty and later give birth to it . . .

Let me show you their dream.
Where Tshimologo, Stevens, Matinki and Ratsoana Jr will run
between our feet . . .
And we later share cheers as we eat.

Let me show you these dreams.
When we would be mesmerized by the sunrise . . . and I,
hypnotized by the sweet warmth of your hazel eyes.

Let me show you my dreams . . .
Or just look in the mirror instead.

## I Became God One Day

God gave me this very fine seed and said,
"I created you, now you create the world."

And I said, "With this fine seed
I will create the ground I stand on and the wind birds glide on.
Hello, my beautiful mustard seed.
Tsoga! Phaphama! For it is time to be strong.
I will bury you. My father's universe will resurrect you.
Oh, no, I am not wrong. You will be strong."

So I became God one day.
Created my mother, designed my father,
Planned my brothers and sisters.
Yes, I gave myself wisdom to create a universe.
But before it began, it had to reverse –
Reverse to a time when I whispered and wrote.
Now I talk and preach but I'm still out of reach.

I became God one day.
Built my bridges and walked my streets.
Wrote my lyrics and germinated my seeds.
Met my wife only to find the one I chose and designed for my life.

I became God only to realize
God is in Us, and Us in Him,
Our hearts direct our paths and our thoughts create our destiny
Through countless preachings and prophesies:
I am his son.
I am God.

## Realizations

We have met
But are still strangers

We have lost
But still possess

We worked hard
But more blood, sweat and tears has to be shed

We marched, dodged bullets and were forced to cry
But are still suffering

It and they come to pass
But we are still living

For love will keep growing
Love will keep knowing

## My 7am Jozi Chariot

White body with shine,
Black shoes like mine,
My chariot makes me smile –
Phela that's Jozi.

100 meter sprints, long distance marathons!
Be careful of your 'interception'
or her hooves and hooter will 'intercept' you!
You know, they talk of her
Like she will one day bury them.
But it's funny how the late and slumberous
Cheer her on as she passes horse and trailer –
Even ponies on the yellow line.

Yes she becomes impatient when you keep her long.
But when she enters and leaves, she chooses her line and rides.
7am Vosloo papa!!

I just slept with her and they start calling with worry and anger.
And they wonder why I drive to school alone.
Zoom-zoom, Mazet stinger –
You all love her but complain when she leaves you.

## Rachel Nokululeko Kalamanye

A young writer from Tsakane in Ekhuruleni, Rachel fell in love with literature in primary school and was active in drama, storytelling and choral verse. She started writing poetry in grade 11 as a way to convey her feelings to those who often misunderstood her. She is an environmental health graduate from the University of Johannesburg and cconsiders the pen and paper the key to her liberation.

## I Wish I Can Own a Club

I wish I owned a club where I can lose myself.
At midnight –the sorceress hour –
I desire to dance with the spirits of the living dead,
Watch witches curse dawn
So when the wolf howls
People are high on life, enchanted,
And worlds collide
And nothing really matters . . .

I want to dance to house music,
Meet my super man on the disco floor
Because I like the way he says my name.
I want to believe in the rhythm of the beats,
Fly high like an eagle because sky's the limit.
I want to go to the Garden of Eden because I have fallen.

I want shadows of the deceased to send messages
That good music is me, the dancer,
Great rhythm is the dj and soul music, life.
I want to make friends and a family on the dance floor
So they will jump at my funeral,
Sing and rejoice: let there be life!

I want to leave footprints on the dance floor –
That's where my destiny will be fulfilled.

# Katlego Maaba

Aka 'Hexed Sante', is a writer, quantity surveying and construction management graduate, dancer, visual artist. An October child from Groblersdal, Tafelkop, Katlego grew up in and around Jo`burg. He started writing at age 14 and has over the past few years formed part of numerous collectives of poets and emcees.

## Note to Poetry

*An official note to poetry to inform of its altering gratifications to life's theory.*

Expressing inadequate truths and eliminating falsely explained lies.
Reconstructing low built sentences into monumental statements that leave towers on history's skyline.
Seeking self-salvation in its existence to redeem the words of lost souls
In a loud voice till they're once again heard.
Contracting expandable terms in scandalous statements
So that even those who fail to perceive meaning can indulge its controversial ambiguities.
Chanting so it may hear the loud spatter in silence's sad cries.
Reviving contained minds, clarifying vague depictions and making them vivid.
Flowing with time and allowing change to ooze in rhymes
and so nourish the mind with thought provoking pace.

**Piece of a note to poetry.**
It may allow the mind to be un-puzzled when it reveals
its true image. . .
If every word completes it,
Then all the worlds' poets will need to imagine strange realities
And factual fictions.

Note to poetry.
You amputated my pen and now my writing is disabled.

Note to poetry.
You changed my life.

## Reply from Poetry

It was never my intention to live in and out of everyone's words.
All I ever was is merely art perfected in verse.
Lyrically I could get worse, metaphysically cause stirs,
Or perhaps in rhymes jump up and down the stairs.
I'm an artist: through your mind, I paint little pictures;
Leave you to realize the image had two faces.
I'm a metaphor: in my structure lines are sentenced
And serve their time by diluting delusions and reversing convulsion.
Love is like a commotion; I touch and stroke hearts
Whilst running my fingers through strands of frail hair.
When I'm spoken, I can repair my victims need to be literate
and mentally prepared.
I live in your words, kiss your lips gently and touch you in spots
that thrust you into pleasure drive.
I never stop loving if you don't stop believing.
The only end I know has full stops.
Having divorced grammar, I'm licensed to free will.
What we had, though just reflection, is depiction of love's
strange reality.
And I've never felt anything so real because I was never matter;
I only thought a great deal.
But then you had me failing for deceit
Till all I could do is repeat eulogies and epics,
Trapping titles unknown 'coz they'd never been written
Having lived in your dreams and held hands
through your nightmare . . .
Sorry I showed little affection and laughed at your lack of perfection.


P.S.  You have beautiful hands – they complement your mind . . .

## Nandiwe Ndawonde

Born on 6 October 1993 and raised in Johannesburg, Sandton. At the age of 3 she started training in ballet (cechetti) and developed a passion for dancing which lead to practicing contemporary dance. Her interest in writing poetry was triggered from the age of 16. Nandiwe is currently a science student (Analytical Chemistry), ballet dancer and poet.

## A Letter to My Mom

Your existence gave birth to a stain
That permanently lives within my heart

Your ambient scarlet love hammered ink
Into my incomplete self of selfishness

Bringing an unconditional moonlight of acceptance
While you paint your joy in my lungs- laughter

Sometimes the carved diamonds you let out
Rust your actions that control my ocean

And the ink I exhale was my personal breath to you.
Love you mom.

## A Letter to my Dad

I am your daughter
You in a different form and type
Hammer my feet to your ground
Marching your name as gravity pulls me
To the core heart you've concealed

Silently blinding my thoughts
I look directly to the sky
That declares you are moonlight
Evaporating my darkness

Sometimes the paint you wear creates the man in me
To stain my ignorance against your word
Flames of rain may rise up
And toughen my memory

You are the man in my life
You have rusted my ways
Rather than becoming a stone from a stone
I linger on the diamond I hunger for.

# Hazel Tobo

Born in Tembisa in 1993 and grew up in Polokwane. Started writing at the age of 11, she also plays the recorder and harmonica and does photography. Hazel has a published book, audio and DVD, under the theme "HAVE WE PUT OUT THE FIRE", compiled together with SHINDIG AWE. She has performed at a number of events around Polokwane, namely Kgorong Poetry and Sound, Woman's Conference, the annual Fire on the Mountain festival in Limpopo and The Next Generation Poetry shows in Melville, Gauteng.

## Sale Souls

Last seen,
A scene caused in the city center.
Cents dance on the concrete,
Singing to their throwing for his drawing,
My reciting,
Sucking off life from my soul.

Cents dance.
Cents, I said,
For a soul poured onto canvas
And mic-less stands.

I sleep missing every night,
Never complete.
And the only way to fill this void
Is to give a piece of my soul every day
To mirrors that only throw my image back at my face –
Those crowds that throw cents.

But I take no offence.
My soul was never erected for sale.

## Fear Lies

Pen, I embrace,
Then yourself, paper,
Planting seeds from my medulla into rich soil –
Soil conceived of my earth; soul . . .

So, self,
I set you on a journey of discovery
For all selves who claim to be captives of poetry.

Dig . . .
Gold is a sign of fancy;

But bones represent life in the earth –
Bones lying naked enrich soil.

Dead poets,
We promised not to lie at your burial
But you lie deep down, many feet under, you lie.

Our inheritance.

## Death is Undeviating

We die not the same death.
But death for mortals arrests in heart attacks,
Or minds stop working – living is nonsense to some;
Death beds cuddle none,
Only some die handsome,
For the very hand that reaches out to all to come
Is the death of one.

You see, the hands of killers remain hands;
Their own blood stains their vessels.
They die, killing each other;
Till then their hearts beat

Printed in the United States
by Baker & Taylor Publisher Services